The Secret of the Wealth Success Chamber: Volume 1

The Secret of the Wealth Success Chamber: Volume 1

Unlock the Gateway to Destiny, Wealth, and Success!

Nikita Lawrence

Acknowledgements

I would first like to thank God in heaven for providing me with the opportunity to serve my family and the world with the gifts placed inside of me. I'm honored to be blessed with the gifts of life and love to truly make an impact by sharing an authentic and genuine love, adding undeniable value to others that results in true transformation.

I would like to thank and honor my awesome and amazing husband for always supporting me and loving me in the way that only he can. Thank you for being patient, kind, caring, understanding, inspiring and just an overall wonderful husband. Thank you for all you do and sacrifice for me and for our family. I get excited when I think about just how much of an unbelievable gift you are; words can't express it. I love you!

I would like to thank my incredible daughter;I'm so honored and grateful that God chose me to be your mommy. Always remember to shine your light baby girl! You are such a gift to our family and to this world! Your personality radiates like the sun, and you light up our world just with your presence alone.

You teach me how to become a better mother every day, and for that, I'm grateful. I look forward to seeing greater success! I love you!

To my mother, thank you for showing me what true resilience looks like. I'm blessed to be your daughter. It's been an honor to watch the blessings from God unfold in your life. Success looks good on you! I will always accept your declaration that God is *sooooooo* faithful as I truly have experienced that in my own life. I love you!

To my three parents, thank you for raising me to be the woman I have grown into today. Thank you for all the sacrifices, lessons learned, good times, and wisdom you have shared with me over the years. Yes, I was both watching and listening! Among other things, you have taught me to work hard, persevere, treat people right, look at the good, and always acknowledge God in everything I do. I love you all!

To my siblings, thank you for allowing me to be the big sister that only I can be. You three are some of the sharpest and most intelligent young adults that I know, and I'm honored to be your sister. I love you all!

To my host of extended family, grandparents (deceased), pastors, spiritual family, friends, acquaintances, and other loved ones, I thank you for anything and everything you taught me. I am better because I have been connected to you and experienced relationships with you. I love and value you all!

Table of Contents

Foreword

What is the Wealth Success Chamber?

The Wealth Success Chamber is the inner court of the soul and spirit, which contains the hidden keys to unlock the gateway to destiny, wealth, and success, accessed only by discovering and demonstrating the identity, purpose, and vision for your life by unlocking the gift of love that begins with you. Additionally, access to your Wealth Success Chamber provides the ability to experience a life of wealth and success holistically through identification, clarity, confidence, and inspiration to achieve goals for life and/or business success.

Who can access the Wealth Success Chamber?

It is my belief that everyone has been granted gifts and talents that God divinely has intricately placed inside the hidden and innermost layers of our spirits, but we must create the right environment for those gifts and talents to be both discovered and cultivated. I don't believe that *anyone* born into this world has been created without one or more gifts and talents. No one is left out! Everyone has access to his or her Wealth Success Chamber, but it must be unlocked by you with the simple choice to say yes to your success.

How does the Wealth Success Chamber enhance my life?

Every gift and talent placed inside of us was placed intentionally with a unique purpose, crafted especially for our lives. When we tap into them, they make room for us, bring us into greatness, and can, if positioned and nurtured correctly, create wealth and both uncommon and tangible success in our lives. Additionally, the Wealth Success Chamber is the catalyst that inspires confidence for aspiring entrepreneurs to take the leap into creating a business that aligns with gifts, talents, passions, and the unique God-given purpose for their lives. It also aids existing entrepreneurs, business leaders, faith leaders, and other leaders in achieving greater success in life and business.

Why haven't others discovered the Wealth Success Chamber?

The problem is that many of us do not go through our lives with an intentional pursuit to discover and cultivate our unique gifts and talents to achieve perfection. Most people simply exist, living mediocre lives and struggling to survive, failing to understand and identify who they are or where they are going, which oftentimes is nowhere fast. The other obstacles that many face that prevent access to the Wealth Success Chamber are emotional toxicity that clouds the mind, heart, and soul and creates paralysis, preventing them from achieving true success.

When is the right time to access the Wealth Success Chamber?

There is no better time to access the Wealth Success Chamber than right now!

How do I access my Wealth Success Chamber?

You can access your Wealth Success Chamber by simply doing the work to unlearn the negative paradigms that have formed your ideas, thoughts, and opinions that have limited your thinking and distorted your perception of who you are and were created to be. Next, you will need to replace those negative and false paradigms with healthy and transformational paradigms that are liberating. In this book, over the next ten days, I will walk with you to reveal the secret and help you access your Wealth Success Chamber by discovering the identity, purpose, and vision for your life.

What is the secret of the Wealth Success Chamber?
If you're like me, you're wondering what *exactly* the secret is. Here it is! The secret of the Wealth Success Chamber is the undeniable truth that *you alone* hold the key to unlock the gift of love inside you to realize the identity, purpose, and vision that permits you to experience the fulfillment of transformation, wealth, and success.

Without dismissing the false labels, lies, fears, and curses of negative self-talk, bitterness, and perpetual cycles of failure from your life, you will not be able to come to a place of honor, acceptance, and transparency that enables you to grow to success and wealth.

Bondage begins in the mind, and to become liberated from the bondage that has kept you in a place of complacency and obscurity, you must be liberated *first* in your mind, and then your decisions, behaviors, and environment will begin to align correctly. Unlocking the gift of love inside you allows you to love, appreciate, honor, embrace, and respect *you* and others around you, thereby creating an atmosphere that positions you for both wealth and success.

Now, are you ready to enter Volume One of *The Secret of the Wealth Success Chamber*?

Please recite the commitment pledge below aloud before moving forward.

Commitment Pledge

I, _____ (*insert your name here*), am determined to experience the manifestation of every hidden promise, gift, talent, vision, and dream that God intelligently placed inside me before my life began. I am certain that my life's existence was no accident and in fact has a significant purpose that is being revealed to me with an undeniable and new sense of clarity and prominence. As I move forward to unveil the innermost layers of my heart, I commit to love, respect, and honor the individual that I was, am, and will be. I am discovering the identity, purpose, and vision for my life to access my very own Wealth Success Chamber. I say to the rest and consequently *best* days, weeks, and years to come in my life, "Triumph, victory, fulfillment, transformation, here I come!"

Your Printed Name: _____

Your Signature:

_____

Date:

_____

Preface

Greetings to you, and welcome to what will be the most exhilarating ten days of your life! Isn't it funny how, at the mention of words like *exhilarating*, our thoughts can instantly make us feel exhausted? If you're thinking, *I'm tired already*, just take a deep breath. Release it. Breathe in deep once more. Now release it, this time more slowly. Maybe I should have welcomed you to "what can be the most *rewarding* ten days of your life"! Ah, there's the calming peace and excitement I was looking for!

If you're like me, you may have scanned through the pages of this book and noticed quite a few pages that are lined and otherwise blank. This was no mistake. No, you don't have the wrong copy. This book is designed to be your partner on your journey and serve as a tool to help you along the way. The blank pages are for you to express and create the design for your future life!

I strongly believe everything you invest in yourself during the next ten days will pay you dividends for the rest of your life. I also recommend that you pace yourself and truly take ten days to examine and apply the principles by exploring one day at a time during our journey.

It will be challenging to make the disciplined choice to refrain from moving ahead, but this will truly be worthwhile and more beneficial in the long run. I am a firm believer that, if you have both consciousness and life, you are equipped with the authority and ability to alter your current life course and direction to truly align with your life purpose and destiny.

If you knew you were just a few steps away from having the life you've always dreamed of or hoped for, would you allow fear or doubt to keep you from taking that first step, or would you take the first step despite fear? Let me be the first to congratulate you on annihilating fear and taking your first step! Your decision to open this book means that you are ready and have everything it takes to move forward on your journey of discovery toward identity, purpose, and vision. Step one is already complete! This is a great place to be encouraged and get a high five from the person sitting next to you. That person may not know why you're asking for a high five, but your radiant smile will be enough for him or her to accept your offer. If you're asked why, just reply, "I am excited about the gift of life and purpose!" Don't worry if there's no one else around; you have permission to high five yourself!

As we progress through the guide, it will be vitally important to establish a few ground rules. These rules are designed to keep you focused and on track and not allow you to sabotage all the progress you will be making. Remember, this is your investment in you.

1. Be open, honest, and transparent.
2. Be authentic and genuine.
3. Celebrate your journey and all successes.
4. Think outside the box.
5. Repeat as often as needed.

Please also note that the bottom of every page has a statement with a blank space for you to fill in information about you:

I love and appreciate this about who I am: _____

This is your commitment to find value in all aspects of who you are as an individual, for *you*! If you find this exercise challenging, please be patient, and remember to look inside your heart to truly see the beauty contained therein.

Day 1

What Is My Current Perspective on My Identity, Purpose, and Vision?

elcome to day one of your journey toward identity, purpose, and vision to access your own Wealth Success Chamber! Whether you are reading in the morning, afternoon, or evening, please accept my warm greeting to you. It is now important for us to gain a foundational alignment with our definition of identity, purpose, and vision. *Identity* can be defined as the combination of one's biological makeup, experiences, environment, character, values, history, and beliefs, the total culmination of a person. The identity of an individual answers the question "Who are you?" *Purpose* can be defined as the overarching reason God put you on Earth and granted your life with existence. The life purpose of an individual answers the question "Why are you here?" *Vision* can be defined as the forward goal and expectation of what will be accomplished. The vision of an individual answers the question "What will you accomplish or achieve?"

Now that we have an aligned definition of identity, purpose, and vision, it is time to get to work! Please take a few moments and write your responses below. Whether you can quickly identify each response or it takes you some time, remember this is your personal journey, and truly, this is no sprint. This is a marathon.

Identity: "Who am I?"

_____
_____
_____
_____
_____
_____

Purpose: "Why am I here?"

_____
_____
_____
_____
_____
_____

Vision: "What will I accomplish?"

_____
_____
_____
_____
_____
_____

Don't worry if you did not really define or articulate everything you hoped you would. In this activity, done is better than perfect." We will revisit this activity near the end of our ten-day journey to reassess and reflect. Congratulations, and thank you for challenging yourself to think beyond the day-to-day complexities of life and truly begin looking inside to reveal more of who you are.

Day One Declaration

I, _____ (*insert full name here*), am excited about my journey to realizing my identity, purpose, and vision by unlocking the gift of love inside me. I am excited and thankful for the gift of life. I have a vision and will fulfill my purpose by knowing my identity and setting clear goals. I commit to making time for me and for embracing the authenticity of who I am. I am moving forward to accomplish everything I ever hoped I would achieve. I am my own success story. I am accessing my Wealth Success Chamber!

My Success Story Reflection Moments

_____

_____

_____

_____

_____

_____

_____

_____

_____

_____

_____

_____

_____

_____

_____

_____

_____

_____

_____

_____

_____

_____

_____

_____

_____

_____

_____

_____

_____

_____

*I love, respect, and appreciate this about who I am:*_____

My Success Story Reflection Moments

_____
_____
_____
_____
_____
_____
_____
_____
_____
_____
_____
_____
_____
_____
_____
_____
_____
_____
_____
_____
_____
_____
_____
_____
_____
_____
_____
_____
_____
_____

*I love, respect, and appreciate this about who I am:*_____

My Success Story Reflection Moments

_____
_____
_____
_____
_____
_____
_____
_____
_____
_____
_____
_____
_____
_____
_____
_____
_____
_____
_____
_____
_____
_____
_____
_____
_____
_____
_____
_____
_____
_____
_____
_____

*I love, respect, and appreciate this about who I am:*_____

Day 2

How Am I Identifying Myself to Others?

*W*elcome to day two of your journey toward identity, purpose, and vision to access your own Wealth Success Chamber. You have *successfully* completed the first day of your personalized life coaching boot camp. Today, we will focus a little more closely on identity. On day one, we aligned our definition of *identity* (a combination of one's biological makeup, experiences, environment, character, values, history, and beliefs, the total culmination of a person; the identity of an individual answers the question "Who are you?"), and you wrote about your self-defined concept of who you are. As individuals, we have different elements of our identity, including, among others, biological, psychological, emotional, spiritual, professional, and financial elements. Each element represents an aspect of our makeup that shapes the totality of who we are or are perceived to be.

In the United States, when people are born, they are given birth certificates and unique Social Security numbers for identification purposes and to ensure they are not mistaken for someone else. Oftentimes in life, we can take on the attributes, thoughts, ideas, and characteristics of someone else, resulting in a less authentic version of ourselves.

While this fact is unfortunately commonplace for many, it leads to a lack of individuality and ultimately may lead to a more dangerous identity crisis.

Some individuals even assume the identity of another person and commit the crime of identity theft for their own personal gain, leaving the person whose identity has been stolen financially and emotionally devastated.

Today, we want to first uncover and define our identity. Let's start by looking at your identity according to how others see you. As frightening as this exercise may sound, I want you to remember the ground rules we set. While perception is reality for many, this exercise of gathering feedback is not intended to shock or attack you in any way. Feedback is truly a gift, and by the end of our journey, you will have gained an appreciation for this gift. This exercise is truly intended to gather information. It will be important for those selected to truly be open and honest with you and to include the good, bad, and otherwise.

Please select three different individuals, and ask them, "How would you describe me to someone else?" They may respond with something like "I think you're great!" If that's the response, please ask them to get into more specifics about your character, personality, and anything else they see in you.

First individual: Who am I to you?

_____

_____

_____

_____

_____

_____

_____

_____

_____

_____

Second individual: Who am I to you?

_____

_____

_____

_____

_____

_____

Third individual: Who am I to you?

_____

_____

_____

_____

_____

_____

Thanks for taking the time to complete step two of the identity exercise! In the upcoming days, we will examine the differences in our attributes and the roles that we play, as well as the relationship between your self-defined identity and how others perceive you. You or others may have described your identity with words like *wife*, *mother*, or *teacher* rather than adjectives that describe your intrinsic qualities.

If you look back and see those words in your first definition from the activity on day one, don't be alarmed. You will have another opportunity at the end of our journey to redefine your identity.

Day Two Declaration

I, _____ (*insert full name here*), am excited about my journey to realizing my identity, purpose, and vision by unlocking the gift of love inside me. I am excited that I was born with an identity and vision, and I will use them both to fulfill my purpose in life. I embrace the intricacies and nuances that make me unique and exude individuality. I acknowledge my strengths and understand that only I can present to myself and the world the best version of *me*! I am my own success story. I am accessing my Wealth Success Chamber!

My Success Story Reflection Moments

_____
_____
_____
_____
_____
_____
_____
_____
_____
_____
_____
_____
_____
_____
_____
_____
_____
_____
_____
_____
_____
_____
_____
_____
_____
_____
_____
_____
_____
_____

*I love, respect, and appreciate this about who I am:*_____

My Success Story Reflection Moments

_____
_____
_____
_____
_____
_____
_____
_____
_____
_____
_____
_____
_____
_____
_____
_____
_____
_____
_____
_____
_____
_____
_____
_____
_____
_____
_____
_____

*I love, respect, and appreciate this about who I am:*_____

My Success Story Reflection Moments

_____
_____
_____
_____
_____
_____
_____
_____
_____
_____
_____
_____
_____
_____
_____
_____
_____
_____
_____
_____
_____
_____
_____
_____
_____
_____
_____
_____
_____
_____
_____

*I love, respect, and appreciate this about who I am:*_____

Day 3

What Is My Personal Brand?

*W*elcome to day three of your journey of discovery of your identity, purpose, and vision to access your own Wealth Success Chamber. You have *successfully* completed the first two days of your personalized life coaching boot camp. Now that you have defined what you believe is your identity, we will now examine the relationship between your self-defined identity and how you are perceived by others. Oftentimes, we may know or have an idea of who we are, but we allow other external factors to prevent us from ensuring that others identify us in the same way. Next, let's go a little deeper and look at the concept of *branding*.

Companies distinguish themselves from their competition in any given industry by creating unique niches, logos, or slogans for their brands. Once a brand has been registered in the United States, its logo and slogan become defined as a *trademark*.

Companies then begin using a variety of marketing techniques to intentionally release their identity, purpose, and vision to the public to attract clients or customers. This is accomplished by ensuring that the trademark reflects the attributes that the company wants customers to identify them with. Additionally, once a brand has been trademarked, no other company is authorized to use the trademark without permission or proper authorization. Any unauthorized usage will result in penalties and hefty fines. In the fast food industry, Burger King and McDonald's have a long-term rivalry. While McDonald's has been the largest fast food chain in the world with the slogan "I'm loving it," Burger King's slogan is "Have it your way." Both food retailers have experienced positive and negative reviews, yet they remain at the top of their industry. In similar fashion, as a person, only you can show the world the best version of *you*! The activity below will explore a few characteristics you would like the world to associate with your brand or trademark.

Please take a moment and reflect on your personal brand. Remember, your brand is how others will identify who *you* are whether you are in a social, professional, spiritual, or leisure environment.

You can be at your best when you have become extremely comfortable with yourself and can present that version of self across all platforms.

Am I asking you to always be "on stage"? I am not asking that you consider yourself to always be on stage, but I am letting you in on a secret:

Every interaction that you have with someone is an opportunity for you to experience his or her brand, just as much as it's an opportunity for you to share yours.

The reality is that people judge character based solely on perception before reality becomes evident.

Others will unfairly prejudge you not based on who you *really* are but on a combination of how you present yourself to them or others and how they draw a comparison to what that has meant in their experience or environment.

Does this mean that someone can falsely perceive you as completely different from who you really are? *Absolutely!* Does this also mean that you must accept accountability and ownership for actions or behaviors you may have knowingly or naively demonstrated that contributed to this perception?

The answer is…yes again. Let's take a moment to reflect on ground rules one and two: (1) be open, honest, and transparent and (2) be authentic and genuine. This is a time where we will be open, honest, transparent, authentic, and genuine.

Remember, this is your time to invest in you. If you just thought of a few experiences or interactions that were neither profitable nor favorable for you, just remember that growth is a process. Moreover, growth can be defined as the process of maturing into something or someone greater than what came before.

In the next exercise, please think about how you would like others to perceive who you are, whether it's the janitor of the company you work for, the company CEO, your child's teacher, your pastor, a sibling, or your closest friend.

Please list the five words that best describe who you are.

1. _____
2. _____
3. _____
4. _____
5. _____

Next, you will come up with a slogan statement to identify who you are. This slogan statement should not have more than seven words or fewer than three words. As you think and reflect on this statement, think of it as what you want others to recognize in you and identify with your name. I've provided an example slogan is for your reference, "Committed to inspiring, empowering, and developing others."

_____
_____
_____

Day Three Declaration

I, _____ (*insert full name here*), am excited about my journey to realizing my identity, purpose, and vision by unlocking the gift of love inside me. I am courageous and excited about the process of growth and development in my life. I embrace the delicate inner workings that make me unique and exquisite as I increase my awareness of my identity. I am strategic and intentional in my expression of myself to the world. I exercise my authority to take ownership of my personal brand and make it authentic so that others experience the *real me*. I am my own success story! I am accessing my Wealth Success Chamber!

My Success Story Reflection Moments

_____
_____
_____
_____
_____
_____
_____
_____
_____
_____
_____
_____
_____
_____
_____
_____
_____
_____
_____
_____
_____
_____
_____
_____
_____
_____
_____
_____
_____
_____

*I love, respect, and appreciate this about who I am:*_____

My Success Story Reflection Moments

_____
_____
_____
_____
_____
_____
_____
_____
_____
_____
_____
_____
_____
_____
_____
_____
_____
_____
_____
_____
_____
_____
_____
_____
_____
_____
_____
_____
_____
_____
_____
_____
_____

*I love, respect, and appreciate this about who I am:*_____

My Success Story Reflection Moments

_____
_____
_____
_____
_____
_____
_____
_____
_____
_____
_____
_____
_____
_____
_____
_____
_____
_____
_____
_____
_____
_____
_____
_____
_____
_____
_____
_____
_____
_____

*I love, respect, and appreciate this about who I am:*_____

Day 4

Have I Passed or Failed the History Test?

*W*elcome to day four of your journey toward identity, purpose, and vision to access your own Wealth Success Chamber! You have *successfully* completed the first three days of your personalized life coaching boot camp. Today is a day of reflection, healing, and discovery as we review all we have learned about identity, purpose, and vision and address past experiences that may have created a false identity.

Many people at some point or another begin a quest for the "true meaning of life." This question sometimes will spin the person into a deeper state of confusion about life. The individual may begin researching death and afterlife experiences; challenging his or her religious belief system; taking risky or spontaneous trips; trying new hobbies or interests; making irresponsible decisions; or using other methods to try to find fulfillment and the answer to the question of meaning.

The quest for the meaning of life may be the result of purpose unfulfilled or a feeling that life isn't "worth living." The quest for the meaning of life may also be the desire to truly have fun and enjoy the pleasures of life. Other times, the quest for the meaning of life may be a coping mechanism to deal with grief or sudden tragedy.

Oftentimes when we experience a series of traumatic events, questions arise. "What am I doing here? What is life about? Why did this happen to me? Where was God? Is God real?" To move forward on our journey, we must dive deeper into the mind to understand the place we are in, our past experiences, and how they have shaped our perception of life and ourselves in this moment.

As a Christian woman of faith, my spiritual views are based on the Holy Bible. I firmly believe the scriptures. One of my favorites states, "God has made all things beautiful in its time." I have seen this in the lives of others and truly experienced it in my own life. As we think about creation, let's look at the transformation of a flowering plant. Flowers begin as seeds and then, with the right ingredients and environment, transition into buds that bloom into beautiful treasures. Flowers are just one example that demonstrates the fulfillment of the scripture of beauty being created from the beginning but apparent in its time. I'm sure that, when we look at a seed, we often are in disbelief that it can and will grow and mature into something greater and more beautiful. The same is true for the caterpillar that morphs into a butterfly. It also holds true for our very lives.

There have been times in my own life when I didn't know or understand how situations would turn out. This was very uncomfortable and quite scary; furthermore, I did not see what beauty would be created at the end of the story. Though I was uncertain of the outcome, I maintained a belief that *everything* I experienced would still ultimately work out for my *good* and glorify my God and Father in heaven. I read this in a scripture and truly embraced the meaning of the words. I can embrace it because those experiences I had, whether they resulted from my naïve or foolish decisions or, in my mind, were undeserved, have contributed to create the whole woman I am today. I now have the ability and desire to help someone else who may be going through or has experienced the things I have faced or other challenges in life. I can now identify anger, hurt, disappointment, despair, depression, loneliness, heartache, and lack of forgiveness. I now can confidently say that we may not always understand why we need to experience some of the things that we go through, but even we when don't understand, we should accept what God allows.

We must trust God's ultimate plan for our lives and that, in the end, what we experience is meant to make us stronger, wiser, and better than we were at the beginning of our journey. The truth is that behind our masks and smiles are stories of life and testimonies of both failure and triumph. Sometimes, however, when we are in the middle of despair, it's hard to see or envision victory.

When experiencing those moments of defeat or anguish, it's imperative to remember to encourage yourself and never miss the lesson learned through the experience. I'm afraid that, for many who experience cycles of the same issue repeatedly, it's because the lesson in that experience was not recognized, so the situation cannot be prevented from occurring again. Our lives were designed for us to make decisions and choices. We must take ownership of those choices whether they are good, bad, right, or wrong. If we don't accept responsibility for or take ownership of *our own* choices, we will remain in despair and never progress to a triumphal state of mind. One lesson to note is that success and triumph begin in the mind before the manifestation is present in reality. We will discuss this further in the upcoming days.

The next exercise below will provide you with the opportunity to journey through your history to reveal different phases in your life and help you gain clarity of how certain events have shaped your current perspective on life including relationships, family, trust, etc. Remember the ground rules. You will not have to share this journal with anyone else, but it is important that you are open and transparent during this exercise because the more you put into it, the more you will gain.

Take a few moments and think about your life. How would you describe it? Explain below.

_____

_____

_____

_____

_____

_____

_____

Think about a time when you felt brilliant or at your best. Describe this time below.

_____

_____

_____

_____

_____

_____

_____

Think about a time when you felt disappointed or hurt. How did you move past that experience? Describe this time below.

_____

_____

_____

_____

_____

_____

_____

Think about a time when you felt like quitting but did not. Describe it below, and include the outcome.

_____

_____

_____

_____

_____

_____

_____

Think about a time or situation that seemed *impossible* to achieve. Describe it below, and include the outcome.

_____

_____

_____

_____

_____

_____

_____

Think about your greatest accomplishments, achievements, or memories during the following spans of time.

Birth to 10 years

_____

10 to 14 years

_____

15 to 19 years

_____

20 to 24 years

_____

25 to 29 years

_____

30 to 34 years

_____

35 to 39 years

_____

40 years +

_____

Think about your greatest mistakes made during the following spans of time.

Birth to 10 years

_____

10 to 14 years

_____

15 to 19 years

_____

20 to 24 years

_____

25 to 29 years

_____

30 to 34 years

_____

35 to 39 years

_____

40 years +

_____

Think about your greatest challenges during the following spans of time.

Birth to 10 years
_____

10 to 14 years
_____

15 to 19 years
_____

20 to 24 years
_____

25 to 29 years
_____

30 to 34 years
_____

35 to 39 years
_____

40 years +
_____

Think about your personal goals for the following spans of time.

18 to 25 years
_____

25 to 35 years
_____

35 to 45 years
_____

45 to 55 years
_____

55 to 65 years

_____

65 years +

_____

Day Four Declaration

I, _____ (*insert full name here*), am excited about my journey to realizing my identity, purpose, and vision by unlocking the gift of love inside me. I embrace the truth about my identity and experiences and how they have affected my life. I acknowledge every decision I have made and take ownership of the outcome of those choices. I forgive myself for the times I disappointed myself and forgive others who have done the same. My past experiences are making me better, not bitter, and I am moving forward into my beautiful future. I am my own success story! I am accessing my Wealth Success Chamber!

My Success Story Reflection Moments

_____

_____

_____

_____

_____

_____

_____

_____

_____

_____

_____

_____

_____

_____

_____

_____

_____

_____

_____

_____

_____

_____

_____

_____

_____

_____

_____

_____

_____

_____

_____

_____

*I love, respect, and appreciate this about who I am:*_____

My Success Story Reflection Moments

_____
_____
_____
_____
_____
_____
_____
_____
_____
_____
_____
_____
_____
_____
_____
_____
_____
_____
_____
_____
_____
_____
_____
_____
_____
_____
_____
_____
_____

*I love, respect, and appreciate this about who I am:*_____

My Success Story Reflection Moments

_____

_____

_____

_____

_____

_____

_____

_____

_____

_____

_____

_____

_____

_____

_____

_____

_____

_____

_____

_____

_____

_____

_____

_____

_____

_____

_____

_____

_____

_____

_____

_____

_____

*I love, respect, and appreciate this about who I am:*_____

Day 5

How Are My Personal Values Governing My Behaviors?

*W*elcome to day five of your journey toward identity, purpose, and vision to access your own Wealth Success Chamber! You have *successfully* completed the first four days of your personalized life coaching boot camp. Today is the day that we celebrate all the progress made during days one through four. I would like to pause and congratulate you on all the effort made to uncover your true identity. Bravo!

Oftentimes, it is much easier to see the identity of others than our own. Some of us may have been raised with the insecurities of our parents or guardians, taught the values they have lived by and deemed appropriate for the time. As we have matriculated into adulthood, we face what our belief system and values are, not based on what we were taught but on our truths, experiences, and exposure.

The reality is that our upbringing, environment, and exposure weigh heavily in the personally defined values that govern our lives. For example, if you were raised in a home with limited or no emotional and financial support, the result may be a deficiency in both giving emotional and financial support to your spouses or children and receiving it from them. This creates a sense of "tough love" and insensitivity to the emotional needs of others based on what you may not have received, which in turn creates yet another deficiency, with you this time being the source. Ouch!

The good news is that we are all empowered to create a new value system for ourselves and our families. Our mind is the most treasured tool that we must use to redefine our perspectives. We will only repeat cycles of deficiencies if we do not stretch and challenge our minds to think beyond what has been taught to us subconsciously. We must fuel our minds with intentional knowledge that perpetuates the truths of our reality or what we want to become our reality. Let's take a closer look at the differences between our current values and our future values. This is the first step in redefining the mind-set that governs how we view ourselves, others, and our lives.

To complete the activity below, please list in order of priority your current values versus the values you want your future life to be governed by. Please number the values with a number from one to seven, with number one being the most important priority and number seven being the least important. Please note, the order in which the values are provided below are in no specific order. Please be 100 percent honest with yourself and number your current values. You will not have to share this with anyone else. After completing your current values, please fill in your future values in order of importance.

Current Values	Future Values
Family	
Work	
Finances	
Spirituality	
Hobbies	
Charity	
Health	

How do you feel about your current values?

_____

_____

_____

_____

_____

_____

_____

How do your current values differ in priority from your future values?

_____

_____

_____

_____

_____

_____

_____

Think about your current life. Now think about the time you spend on various activities. Does your time spent align (in quality and quantity) with the order of importance you noted above? (For example, if hobbies are your number seven priority, do you spend more time on hobbies than you do with charity if charity is your number five priority?) Please explain.

_____
_____
_____
_____
_____
_____
_____

How do you want your time spent to differ from how you're currently spending it?

_____
_____
_____
_____
_____
_____
_____

What are some ways you can make a few changes to reorder your time and align it closer to your future values?

1. _____
2. _____
3. _____
4. _____
5. _____

Thank you for completing the activity above! This activity may have taken longer than you anticipated, but you truly looked deeply within to uncover some hidden truths that are governing your current behaviors. In the upcoming days, we will look more closely at the concept of time and how to use it to your benefit and not have it used against you. The key to managing your time in alignment with your values is to ensure the proper balance of both quality and quantity.

Day Five Declaration

I, _____ (*insert full name here*), am excited about my journey to realizing my identity, purpose, and vision by unlocking the gift of love inside me. I am empowered to take control of my life by making intentional choices to live the life I desire. I accept the values that add meaning and virtue to my life. I accept the lessons learned through both good and bad experiences and commit to breaking any unhealthy perspectives that lead to deficiencies in my mind, my life, or the lives of my family members. I accept my responsibility to be the change I want to see and look forward to the process of growth in every area of my life. I am a success story! I am accessing my Wealth Success Chamber!

My Success Story Reflection Moments

_____

_____

_____

_____

_____

_____

_____

_____

_____

_____

_____

_____

_____

_____

_____

_____

_____

_____

_____

_____

_____

_____

_____

_____

_____

_____

_____

_____

_____

*I love, respect, and appreciate this about who I am:*_____

My Success Story Reflection Moments

_____
_____
_____
_____
_____
_____
_____
_____
_____
_____
_____
_____
_____
_____
_____
_____
_____
_____
_____
_____
_____
_____
_____
_____
_____
_____
_____
_____
_____

*I love, respect, and appreciate this about who I am:*_____

My Success Story Reflection Moments

_____

_____

_____

_____

_____

_____

_____

_____

_____

_____

_____

_____

_____

_____

_____

_____

_____

_____

_____

_____

_____

_____

_____

_____

_____

_____

_____

_____

_____

*I love, respect, and appreciate this about who I am:*_____

Day 6

Who and What Have I Allowed to Taint or Distort My Self-Image?

Welcome to day six of your journey toward identity, purpose, and vision to access your own Wealth Success Chamber! You have *successfully* completed the first five days of your personalized life coaching boot camp. Today will be a day of reflection and reaffirming. The last five days have truly been days of discovery, uncovering and unmasking the core of who we truly are as individuals. Today's focus will be on self-image and self-esteem.

The images we see around us have greatly affected our perceptions of beauty and what is acceptable or unacceptable, attractive or unattractive. From the youngest ages in childhood, many of us have been conditioned to see beauty very superficially.

The perception of physical beauty, often defined by the compliments or insults of others, have left many wounded even several years later with lasting scars that have not healed. It's amazing how words can so quickly leave the mouth and create damage that truly is nearly impossible to repair. Many of us can recall and vividly remember some of the hurtful things that have been said to or about us even as children, though we may now be middle-aged.

The reality is that the hurtful words spoken to or about us have contributed to some of the insecurities that we may still be facing today and are *still* hindering us from truly embracing the wholeness of our identity. The words that define physical appearance, such as *pretty*, *cute*, *handsome*, *ugly*, *unattractive*, and so forth, are all relative to the preferences of the individual making the statement and drawing the conclusion.

Most of us have heard the adage "Beauty is in the eye of the beholder," and I would firmly agree with that statement. God, in His infinite wisdom and knowledge, created everyone with a unique sparkle, twinkle, feature, and gift. I wholeheartedly believe that everyone is beautiful in his or her own unique way.

Have you ever seen a couple that you felt was mismatched? Did one seem too attractive to be truly dedicated and in love with the other, whom you personally find less attractive or undeserving? What made that other person so unattractive in your opinion? Where did you learn or decide that those features or characteristics were unbecoming and undesired? Was this taught, or is it a personal preference for you? Have you ever found someone attractive that your friends or family members just did not find attractive? Did you continue to have the same level of attraction, or did it begin to fade or diminish?

Clothes are designed for a variety of different tastes but with a specific style in mind. The individuals selecting a clothing item must see the value and perceive it as complementary to "the look" they're pursuing to deem the item beautiful or a "must have." It is the same with attraction. What works for one does not work for all. Just because someone didn't find you attractive doesn't mean that you are not attractive and beautiful. It's just unfortunate that this individual or group couldn't see your beauty and value. If you've never been told before, let me be the first to say, "You are incredibly attractive and gorgeous, both fearfully and wonderfully made by God and in his image and likeness! Every physical feature you have was designed to express your individual uniqueness and exquisiteness."

Today is the day that we together dismantle and come out of agreement with every hurtful word spoken to you that has crippled and blinded you, preventing you from truly embracing the beauty of who you are. Today we peel back the scales on your eyes to truly look from the outside to the inside to redefine the beauty that has always been *you*. In this moment, let's take the opportunity to release all the emotion and negative energy that has been masked and buried under the layers of our outer "tough" shell. Let's also release the people who are partly responsible for creating the damage. To release both the emotion and those responsible, we must consciously make the choice to freely grant forgiveness. We won't be able to move forward and see our true selves in a genuine way until we forgive those who planted the seeds of insecurity and inferiority. The reality is that, while they may have planted the seeds, we ourselves watered and allowed them to grow into the weeds that currently exist in our hearts. The good news is that we can acknowledge and uproot those weeds to truly move forward in freedom, no longer hindered in the present and future by our past but liberated to embrace the journey of life that has brought us to this moment of realization of our true worth, value, and magnificence.

We will now move forward into an activity that will allow you to express your thoughts about both your inner and physical beauty.

Take two photos of yourself, one face shot and one full-body shot. Below each image, describe seven physical attributes that you find beauty in.

INSERT FULL-BODY SHOT PHOTO IMAGE HERE	INSERT HEAD SHOT PHOTO IMAGE HERE

1. _____
2. _____
3. _____
4. _____
5. _____
6. _____
7. _____

Please describe the outcome of the activity above. How did you feel describing your beauty? Did you find seven attributes that you find beautiful? Why or why not? Did this make you uncomfortable? Why or why not?

_____

_____

_____

_____

_____

_____

_____

In the next activity, we will look at the internal qualities that make you beautiful. Draw pictures inside the heart of what makes you happiest and filled with joy. Below the heart, list seven internal qualities that you find beautiful.

1. _____
2. _____
3. _____
4. _____
5. _____
6. _____
7. _____

Describe the outcome of the activity above. How did you feel describing your beauty? Did you find seven internal qualities that you find beautiful? Why or why not? Did this make you uncomfortable? Why or why not?

_____
_____
_____
_____
_____
_____
_____

Day Six Declaration

I, _____ (*insert full name here*), am excited about my journey to realizing my identity, purpose, and vision by unlocking the gift of love inside me. I reaffirm my value and beauty both inside and outside from a place of authentic love, not vanity. I dispel all ill and negative thoughts of myself from my mind and heart. I come into agreement with the realization that I am a wonderful creation of God, designed to reflect the splendor of His goodness, faithfulness, and love. I respect myself and have a favorable impression of the individual I see in my reflection. I am liberated to fully *love* the individual I am both inside and out and will show that love to those around me as I embrace my identity and fulfill my destined purpose. I am a success story! I am accessing my Wealth Success Chamber!

My Success Story Reflection Moments

_____
_____
_____
_____
_____
_____
_____
_____
_____
_____
_____
_____
_____
_____
_____
_____
_____
_____
_____
_____
_____
_____
_____
_____
_____
_____
_____
_____
_____
_____
_____

*I love, respect, and appreciate this about who I am:*_____

My Success Story Reflection Moments

_____
_____
_____
_____
_____
_____
_____
_____
_____
_____
_____
_____
_____
_____
_____
_____
_____
_____
_____
_____
_____
_____
_____
_____
_____
_____
_____
_____
_____
_____

*I love, respect, and appreciate this about who I am:*_____

My Success Story Reflection Moments

_____
_____
_____
_____
_____
_____
_____
_____
_____
_____
_____
_____
_____
_____
_____
_____
_____
_____
_____
_____
_____
_____
_____
_____
_____
_____
_____
_____

*I love, respect, and appreciate this about who I am:*_____

Day 7

How Does True Forgiveness Create Freedom and Liberty while Bitterness Perpetuates Cycles of Bondage and Misery?

*W*elcome to day seven of your journey of identity, purpose, and vision to access your own Wealth Success Chamber! You have *successfully* completed the first six days of your personalized life coaching boot camp. I am so excited about the progress you have made, along with the effort you have put into the discovery of your identity. By this point, you may have found yourself grabbing a few tissues (or many more than a few), closing the journal to return later, or even considering giving up because of the magnitude of the emotional learning of the last six days. (If you haven't completed all activities for days one through six, I sincerely ask that you *stop* and go back. Don't worry how long it takes or how difficult it feels; just keep pressing forward no matter what.) This journey of identity discovery is the foundation for purpose and vision. The understanding needed to ascertain your purpose will not be fully awakened without the fundamental knowledge of your core identity.

I want you to know I am extremely proud of you and the progress you have made. Anytime we are creating a new paradigm that challenges the way we have thought or, much more, how we have viewed ourselves, much work, effort, and energy are required.

The wonderful aspect of learning and growing in knowledge and wisdom is that the information garnered can never be removed from your mind. You can try to revert to the old way of thinking, but your inner conscientiousness will not allow you to comfortably make that transition. Even more, you picked up this book to challenge yourself to achieve more than what you had before *and* you have decided to move *forward*, so that is what we will continue to do!

During the activity of day six, we explored self-esteem. Today we will look deeper into the principle of forgiveness. Forgiveness can be defined as the act of releasing a person or persons from an offense.

The pardon is offered with a statement like "I'm sorry" or "I apologize," but less often does the statement include the question "Will you forgive me?" Some will make their apology, "Please forgive me," as a declarative statement, not a question that requires an actual response.

Many of us have been taught that the appropriate response to such statements should be a gracious "That's ok" or "Yes, I forgive you."

But what happens when the offense is not followed by the aforementioned statements, and in your heart you truly feel a slow bubbling that surfaces to say, "Well, no, I really don't forgive you. What you did was truly not ok"? Or what happens when the person who caused the offense does not even stop to acknowledge it by offering an apology? Is withholding your forgiveness the right thing to do in response? Is remaining angry or holding a grudge appropriate even if it is seemingly deserved?

The answer is no, it is not. Throughout the many experiences I have lived through, I have learned one fundamental truth about forgiveness: forgiveness is for *you*, not *them*! We often walk around holding on to the hurt, resulting in what we believe is a justifiable grudge against the other person or persons. Ultimately, such a grudge is really a personal attack against ourselves and our own peace of mind.

Unfortunately, the reality is that what we believe we are entitled to feel against those who have caused us hurt feelings, pain, disappointment, suffering, or turmoil will only successfully create a more destructive mental and emotional state of mind than before.

I am not saying that we should overlook or disregard the true depth of the wrongs we have experienced, but I am saying that we must get to a place where the effects of those injuries no longer have the ability to negatively affect our temperament in *our own lives*. Forgiveness doesn't validate what the other person did or didn't do, but it does liberate you to *move forward* and not remain stuck in the wounded place of hurt. The life we have been blessed to experience here on Earth is the *only* one we have, and it's up to us to seize this opportunity and make the most of it; after all, it belongs to *us*!

Because we only get one shot to live our best and greatest lives, why waste the limited time that we have forever experiencing the emotional distress and baggage of lack of forgiveness? When God created us as human beings, he gave us the authority to take control of our thoughts, perspectives, and emotions. This includes not giving over our present peace and future joy to situations and people that were never designed to understand our true value or worth. Furthermore, we don't deserve to live under the curse of lack of forgiveness, destroying our future because of our past experiences. We must learn to find the purpose and value in every situation we have encountered so that we can continue growing and maturing versus merely getting older.

One last fundamental truth about forgiveness is that *only* we can exercise it, and this isn't something that *anyone* can do for us. Just take a moment and think about it.

Can a mother's forgiveness of the first boyfriend who broke her daughter's heart replace the forgiveness that the daughter needs to demonstrate to that boyfriend so she can be liberated to move forward in life? We may have people in our lives who urge and encourage us to take the step toward forgiveness but they cannot forgive on our behalf. As individuals, we must exercise ownership of our role and accept responsibility for ourselves and our actions. We must make the choice to be liberated through forgiveness. The good news is that, once we make the choice to demonstrate forgiveness as a value and not a chore, it becomes easier and easier to maintain an atmosphere of serenity. Essentially, if we choose to remain in lack of forgiveness or continue holding grudges, we are also choosing to remain in bondage to the emotional damage of the situation or individual that caused the hurt. We need to love ourselves enough to choose to become better and not bitter individuals.

In the exercise below, you will dig a little deeper into the areas of your heart to unmask the wounds of lack of forgiveness and allow healing to permeate your heart and mind so that you are no longer injured or wounded in the deepest fibers of your innermost selves. Remember, this is your personal assessment, so be 100 percent honest with yourself; be true.

True or False Quiz (Circle One)

I have always felt loved, respected, and accepted by my family.
    True   False

I have always felt loved, respected, and accepted by my close friends.
    True   False

I have never experienced rejection, loss, disappointment, or regret.
    True   False

I have never experienced someone close to me being dishonest or untruthful.
    True   False

I have never experienced someone close to me breaking a promise or vow.
    True   False

I quickly forgive others anytime I take offense to their behavior.
    True   False

I forgive others who have wronged me or others close to me only if they offer an apology.

    True   False

I always forgive myself for the times that I disappoint myself or make the wrong decisions.

    True   False

I do not embrace (have present feelings of) guilt or shame for the mistakes of my past.

    True   False

I do not currently hold a grudge against anyone.

    True   False

In the section below, describe how this exercise made you feel. As you moved through each section, what experiences came to mind?

_____

_____

_____

_____

_____

_____

_____

How many responses did you mark as true? How many as false? Did any responses surprise you? Why?

_____

_____

_____

_____
_____
_____
_____

Who do you still need to forgive? Why?

_____
_____
_____
_____
_____
_____

What areas do you still need to forgive yourself in? Please explain.

_____
_____
_____
_____
_____
_____

In what areas are you personally ashamed of?

_____
_____
_____
_____
_____
_____

I'm so proud of the transparency you have shown to the man or woman in the mirror. To move forward, you must come to the realization of exactly where you stand.

I realize this exercise was intense, and you may have found moments of questioning whether you would truly open yourself up to facing the reality of lack of forgiveness in your heart. I applaud you for making the hard but necessary decision. If you did not complete the activity above with 100 percent *truth*, please *stop* and revisit it.

We won't be able to move forward together without this critical principle of forgiveness. You may have answered more questions with a response of false than you expected, and that is ok. That doesn't make you a bad person; it just makes you human. Now that you are aware, the question is "What are you going to do about it?"

Always remember that forgiveness is a choice, but healing is a process. Forgiveness is for you, and it *does not* validate the wrong or hurt you experienced because of someone else's inability to make the right choices. The old adage that "time heals all wounds" is a fallacy! Time doesn't heal any wound you haven't forgiven.

It has been my personal experience that I can make the choice to forgive, but then I must pray and ask God to heal my heart so that I am no longer living with the effects of the hurt I experienced. I have known God to truly be a healer, deliverer, and redeemer.

Always remember that God, not time, heals all wounds. As He perfects the healing in your heart and mind, you must embrace the reality that He *allowed* you to experience some of the things you did so that He could show his glory in and through you to help someone else. During the darkest moments of our lives, we feel as if we cannot even help ourselves, let alone anyone else. If that is how you have felt before or are feeling now, this chapter is *just for you*! It's in our weakest moments that we can pull on the strength of God to endure and press forward to embrace our future.

Now, let's pause for a few moments and reflect on your life. Reflect on the good, the bad, sorrow, joy, tragedy, and triumphs. Meditate on the realization that everything you have experienced in life has brought you to this very moment. Though you may not be where you hoped or wished you would be by now, you *are* in the right place at the right time, reading the right book, experiencing the very breakthrough you need to get into position and take control of your thoughts, feelings, emotions, choices, and self-image.

All those factors combined, healthy or unhealthy, are currently determining your view of yourself and, consequently, the identity you project to the world.

Just think: someone somewhere is waiting to experience the glorious person inside of *you*! Only you can unlock the gift of magnificence that was placed inside you before you born. Now it's time to release the excess baggage of lack of forgiveness and embrace the luxurious freedom that is your right!

Take a few moments and reflect on everyone who comes to mind when you think about those you haven't forgiven, including yourself. This next exercise is critical. Please select a friend or person of whom you trust who will not be judgmental but trusted to love you, embrace you, and experience the nakedness of your vulnerability. It's best to complete exercise in person, but it can be done via phone or electronic device if an in-person visit is not feasible. Please create your forgiveness list and separate the person from the situation and the outcome of his or her actions that you have held in offense. Next, the declarative statements that you make must be spoken aloud and not within your mind.

Choose your forgiveness by making the statement below using your voice.

Forgiveness Statement
"(*Insert his/her name here*), I acknowledge you, the hurt you have caused me, the situation, and the aftermath. I acknowledge the pain I have experienced because of your choices and my own. I acknowledge my own choice to mask or remain in the place of hurt. I now loose the effects of the hurt and ask God for healing for both you and me. I choose forgiveness because I know that I am imperfect and deserve forgiveness. I forgive you. I no longer hold you or me in bondage to the mistakes of the past. I choose forgiveness even if you don't see or acknowledge that you ever did anything wrong. I forgive you. I now embrace my freedom from the prison that existed in my mind and the false reality that I could not or would not be able to move forward because of this. I forgive myself."

Repeat the exercise above as many times as needed based on the number of people needing forgiveness. No matter how long it takes, you should continue to repeat this declaration, as it is essential for progress. Remember, it is crucial that everyone and each situation is acknowledged using the above statement.

Forgiveness doesn't always mean that you will no longer remember every situation, but it does mean that you may find that you can no longer recall certain details as vividly, and the emotion behind the situation may no longer affect you as it did when it occurred.

Day Seven Declaration

I _____ (*insert full name here*) am excited about my journey to realizing my identity, purpose, and vision by unlocking the gift of love inside me. I am grateful for the opportunity to explore the hidden areas of my heart and mind that only I may know exists. I embrace the strength I have within to make the hard choices that are right. I am competent and capable, and I acknowledge my responsibility to hold myself accountable. I intentionally forgive myself and others anytime I experience hurt or disappointment. I come out of agreement with self-pity and having a victim's mentality. I come into agreement with the mind-set of victory and purposely choose triumph over tragedy. I recognize that I have experienced both in my life and now am on the path to success, not failure. I am excited about my future and unlocking the gifts inside me that will positively affect the world. I am my own success story! I am accessing my Wealth Success Chamber!

My Success Story Reflection Moments

_____

_____

_____

_____

_____

_____

_____

_____

_____

_____

_____

_____

_____

_____

_____

_____

_____

_____

_____

_____

_____

_____

_____

_____

_____

_____

_____

_____

_____

_____

_____

_____

*I love, respect, and appreciate this about who I am:*_____

My Success Story Reflection Moments

_____

_____

_____

_____

_____

_____

_____

_____

_____

_____

_____

_____

_____

_____

_____

_____

_____

_____

_____

_____

_____

_____

_____

_____

_____

_____

_____

_____

_____

_____

_____

*I love, respect, and appreciate this about who I am:*_____

My Success Story Reflection Moments

_____
_____
_____
_____
_____
_____
_____
_____
_____
_____
_____
_____
_____
_____
_____
_____
_____
_____
_____
_____
_____
_____
_____
_____
_____
_____
_____
_____
_____
_____
_____

*I love, respect, and appreciate this about who I am:*_____

Day 8

How Does Fear Alter My Perception of My Personal Worth or Value?

elcome to day eight of your journey to realizing your iden-tity, purpose, and vision to access your own Wealth Success Chamber! Congratulations! You have *successfully* completed the first seven days of your personalized life coaching boot camp. Let's take a moment to reflect.

How are you feeling? What's on your mind? How would you describe the past seven days in twenty words or less?

_____
_____
_____
_____
_____
_____
_____

As promised, you may be feeling the intensity of the emotional learning that has been required, but I applaud you for stepping up to the plate. Not only did you prove to yourself that you are capable of accomplishing what you set your mind to do but you have also demonstrated your tenacity to achieve success while doing so. Let me remind you today that you were born to be *remarkable*, not insignificant. Failure is a mind-set. Mediocrity is a choice. Procrastination is fatal. Excellence is attainable. Greater success is imminent. Your life is extraordinarily *valuable*, has *meaning*, and is *needed*.

Today we will dive into the principle of understanding your value and worth as an individual. Oftentimes, we look for others to esteem us or determine what our value is, rather than assuming a position of authority in our own lives and informing others of our value. Why is that? Who told us what we could or couldn't have? What we did or didn't deserve? What we would or wouldn't achieve? Who planted the seeds of doubt and fear and diminished our dreams? When did our ideas become fairy-tale stories that we thought we could only read about in books or watch for entertainment in movies? Where in our lives did success become such a fleeting fantasy? Take a few moments and really reflect on the questions above. These are not rhetorical questions but questions that we need to answer to ourselves, if *no one else*.

Please use the space below to provide your response. No matter how long it takes, take the time needed to determine the answers; FYI, "I don't know" is *not* an appropriate response. Ouch!

The reason it is important to understand where we lost hope in ourselves is that we will need to rebuild and restore hope from that place in the past for the sake of our future. For some, the inadequacy began at school with being chosen last for games during gym classes, having to sit alone in the cafeteria for lunch, or being bullied or made fun of. For some, the inadequacy began in childhood with an absent parent. For some, the rejection continued with not having a date for school functions or dances and not understanding why. For others, this cycle of rejection and inadequacy continued to grow with breakups of romantic relationships, divorces, or even struggles with infertility or miscarriages. These feelings of unworthiness, rejection, and abandonment, when they are not dealt with, snowball into a completely catastrophic monster of *fear.*

Fear is a deadly weapon that will paralyze you and prevent you from any type of progress if you allow it to rule your life. The very thought of things that are frightening to us sometimes will take our very breath away. Isn't that interesting?

Even more interesting is understanding that fear disguises itself in many forms: negativity, anxiety, pride, arrogance, mediocrity, low/no expectations, hopelessness, complacency, withdrawnness, false identity, and indecisiveness are just a few.

Do you recognize any of these forms of fear taking residence and creating a home in your life? Often, fear will fall into three categories based on the situations in our lives: fear of staying, fear of leaving, and fear of the unknown. Another way to describe these categories is fear of things remaining the same, fear of things changing, and fear of the future. The reality is that the emotion of fear invokes the idea that something is either a threat or danger to us even if that threat or danger is imaginary and *does not actually exist.* Wow! In essence, some of the things we are fearful of were completely imagined and were never designed to play a part in our lives as a reality.

When I was a child, my father often spoke of Murphy's law: "What can go wrong will go wrong." Whenever he referenced this "law," he and I would share many laughs and stories where it truly appeared to be the reality of what occurred. It became one of the staples of our jokes until I became old enough to reference it myself. Though we used this "law" in humor, if I had not been careful and had truly internalized it as a universal law in my life, I would have been giving fear a home in my life.

There is a major difference between fear of the unknown and proper planning. Proper planning is a critical principle for responsible living. Don't confuse proper planning and being responsible with experiencing fear and making decisions based on that fear. For example, life insurance is a decision of responsibility, while not pursuing the career of your choice or starting your dream business may be a decision of fear. Please note that timing is certainly a critical element that must be carefully evaluated before making any major life changes that will affect your family and livelihood. However, always remember that, if you are not moving forward, you are falling behind. Yikes!

Just think about the very concept of time. Time is constant, moving forward with every second of the day. We know that there are twenty-four hours in a day and that we don't have the ability to freeze time the way we can hit the pause button on movies or live TV shows with today's technology.

Look at your life. How has fear stolen valuable time from your pursuit of greatness and success? The bad news is that fear may have stolen years of valuable time from our lives. The great news is that now, as we are taking responsibility for our decision to allow fear to reside in our emotions and consequently drive our choices, we also have the power to change.

We have both the authority and ability to eradicate it from our emotions and decisions so that it can no longer continue robbing our gifts from God: life and precious time. Furthermore, when we come out of agreement with allowing fear to govern our emotions and choices, we create the space for our value to be recognized and revealed both to ourselves and to the world.

In the exercise below, please list ten goals that you want to accomplish in your lifetime and when and why you want to accomplish them. Before you begin this exercise, please take a moment and quiet your mind. You must remove every limitation and barrier in your mind that says you could or would *never* be able to accomplish this or that. As a reminder, accessing your Wealth Success Chamber includes being able to live a life of wealth and success holistically by taking the action to identify and establish clarity with your personal success goals.

Please complete the exercise 100 percent and remember, your responses regarding when and why are just as important as the goals themselves. There is no goal is silly, too big, too hard, or even impossible. Remember, *every* goal is attainable with the right mind-set, plan, and actions. A key fundamental principle of having the right mind-set is ensuring that your spiritual mind lines up with the Holy Bible.

Goals	When	Why
1. _____	_____	_____
2. _____	_____	_____
3. _____	_____	_____
4. _____	_____	_____
5. _____	_____	_____
6. _____	_____	_____
7. _____	_____	_____
8. _____	_____	_____
9. _____	_____	_____
10. _____	_____	_____

In the exercise below, please list your current and desired career occupations and income, both hourly and annually. Remember, your desired income reflects your value, worth, and results that are delivered by you, not your current paycheck. This amount mirrors your education, experience, work ethic, creativity, and ability to make an impact. This amount should be a measurement of the results you achieve for the company. I ran across great wisdom in a very profound statement: "Someone's lack of resources doesn't define or determine my value." In the same manner, someone's lack of resources doesn't determine your value. Keep that in mind as you fill in your desired wage and salary.

Current Occupation _____
Current Hourly Wage $_____/hour
Current Annual Salary $_____/year
Desired Occupation _____
Desired Hourly Wage $_____/hour
Desired Annual Salary $_____/year

Today's lesson was not meant to suggest that you will never experience fear of anything. We all fear something at some point. The purpose of today's lesson is to create a more definite awareness of your value and worth in your own eyes and to dismantle the mindset of fear continuing to hide and reside in your thoughts and decisions. We must conquer fear with action and progress. Progress is the enemy of and antidote for fear. Stagnation, a lack of forward motion, is the drug that keeps fear alive. The reality is that, if we don't begin to look at our dreams in life as goals with expected dates of accomplishment and begin preparing plans and specific actions, we will never see progress. Whatever you set out to do, no matter how big the goal is, no matter how afraid you may be feeling, *do it anyway*. Move forward *afraid* if you need to; just start moving forward so you don't continue falling behind.

Day Eight Declaration

I, _____ (*insert full name here*), am excited about my journey to realizing my identity, purpose, and vision by unlocking the gift of love inside me. I am grateful for the opportunity to change the course of my life from governing my decisions from a place of fear to a position of *fearlessness*. I come out of agreement with fear, negativity, anxiety, complacency, stagnation, indecisiveness, and doubt. I shake loose the effects of fear in my life. I embrace the confidence and certainty of my value and greatness inside. I no longer embrace self-pity but take full responsibility for my choices that brought me where I am currently in life. I come into agreement with progress and forward movement toward my destined life of success that lies ahead. I am my own success story! I am accessing my Wealth Success Chamber!

My Success Story Reflection Moments

_____
_____
_____
_____
_____
_____
_____
_____
_____
_____
_____
_____
_____
_____
_____
_____
_____
_____
_____
_____
_____
_____
_____
_____
_____
_____
_____
_____
_____

*I love, respect, and appreciate this about who I am:*_____

My Success Story Reflection Moments

_____
_____
_____
_____
_____
_____
_____
_____
_____
_____
_____
_____
_____
_____
_____
_____
_____
_____
_____
_____
_____
_____
_____
_____
_____
_____
_____
_____
_____
_____

*I love, respect, and appreciate this about who I am:*_____

My Success Story Reflection Moments

_____
_____
_____
_____
_____
_____
_____
_____
_____
_____
_____
_____
_____
_____
_____
_____
_____
_____
_____
_____
_____
_____
_____
_____
_____
_____
_____
_____
_____
_____
_____

*I love, respect, and appreciate this about who I am:*_____

Day 9

How Do I Take Ownership to Improve after Failure?

Welcome to day nine of your journey to realizing your identity, purpose, and vision to access your own Wealth Success Chamber. Congratulations on successfully completing the first eight days of your personalized life coaching boot camp. Yesterday's lesson revealed the obstacle called "fear" that prevents the actualization of self-worth and value. This only occurs if fear is left to continue residing in your mind, emotions, choices, and behavior. As we continue to discuss the principle of conquering fear to achieve progress, wealth, and success, another obstacle that tries to stand in your way is the very thought of failure. Self-efficacy is most often defined as your personal belief about your ability and capacity to achieve or accomplish something. Today we will explore failure, as yesterday, we learned that failure is a mind-set. To stay liberated from fear and demonstrate fearlessness, we must understand the crucially important truth about how we are conditioning our minds.

It is through our thinking or thought paradigm that our emotions are shaped, and then they directly guide our behaviors, decisions, inclinations, progression, stagnation, or regression. Our beliefs, perspectives, and perception of life and our life experiences will truly determine our trajectory and determine our ability to achieve sustained success. Take a few moments and ponder that statement.

Think about some of the situations or circumstances have faced throughout your life. Think about your joys, triumphs, and greatest accomplishments. Please share your thoughts below.

_____
_____
_____
_____
_____
_____
_____

Now let's look at the other end of the spectrum. Think about your greatest feelings of defeat. Think about times when you felt you'd hit rock bottom and wouldn't be able to recover. Think about times when you thought you'd had lost everything and didn't have the strength to start over or rebuild.

_____
_____
_____
_____
_____
_____
_____

One fundamental truth is that, while every situation may not yield the desired end result, or perhaps you now see mistakes that could have been easily prevented, as long as you live, you will experience both triumphs and opportunities to learn, grow, and become both better and wiser.

While the definition of failing is truly not receiving the desired outcome in a situation, the truth is that failing doesn't make you a *failure*.

Experiencing failure and becoming a failure are crucially different, yet many allow the stigma of becoming a failure based on a failed experience to keep them in this dreadful place of bondage. Every mistake, bad decision, immature action, and so forth that you have made doesn't have to become the sum total of your identity and *does not alone define you*. You hold the power to make this a reality or fleeting fantasy. To avoid being defined by the less than desirable history of your past, you must learn to embrace the lessons learned as a result of those actions or behaviors and improve *because, not in spite of it*. Friends, it's very easy to shout to the mountaintops, "I made it, despite this or that," but it's a more sobering feat to say, "I made it because of this and that." Some of our most painful experiences have also given us our greatest teachings and wisdom to embrace and live by.

Take a few moments and write down a few of the hardest or most painful lessons you've learned. This exercise may take longer than a few moments, and that is perfectly ok. Take the time to dig deep, and don't rush through it. This exercise is crucial as we move forward.

_____

_____

_____

_____

_____

_____

_____

_____

_____

_____

Write down your reactions to the exercise above. Was it difficult? How long did it take? Did it take longer than you initially thought it would? Are you surprised by what you've learned from your life?

_____

_____

_____

_____

_____

_____

_____

The book of Genesis in the Bible speaks of the origin of creation and the establishment of seasons on the earth. This scripture revealed to me that, just as the seasons and the weather change, so we experience summer, fall, winter, and spring, and so will our lives experience different seasons. We will experience joy, pain, triumph, disappointment, new beginnings, and some endings. Just as the moon glows at night and the sun radiates to announce the dawning of another day, so does each moment and day offer the gift of opportunity.

This opportunity is the chance we have been given to become even more improved versions of ourselves than we were yesterday or the day or week or month or years before. Isn't that exciting? The key is in realizing that you hold the power to shape your future, not based on the history of your past but on your purpose and the desires of your heart for your life, legacy, and ultimately your destiny. Please understand that you will ascertain your purpose and have the courage to pursue destiny *only* after deciding not to allow your past circumstances, thoughts, mistakes, history, and so forth to define your future as a limited, negative, and misguided average or below-average person.

You must redefine your view of both your present and future self in a healthy, vibrant, and positive way to successfully transition out of the damaging curses that lie within the thoughts that float through your mind and heart.

Take a few moments and write down your redefined view of first your present and then your future. Please be sure that this description is a positive, healthy, and vibrant depiction of your life.

_____
_____
_____
_____
_____
_____
_____

What do you want to accomplish and leave as a legacy by the end of your life's journey? Please take a few moments and provide your response in the space below.

_____
_____
_____
_____
_____
_____
_____

Let me ask you another question. If you knew that, to accomplish the vision you have just described above, it would cost you everything you have, would you be willing to sacrifice it? Are you willing to let go of what you had to embrace the greater dimensions of what you have not yet experienced? Are you willing to release the old mind-set, negativity, hurt, disappointment, lack of forgiveness, isolation, complacency, procrastination, and uncertainty of your past to embrace the beauty of and confidence in the successful future that awaits?

If someone told you that the process required to reach the vision described above will require two business failures before you journey to the business idea that secures your financial stability for your entire family and every generation following, would you still take the leap?

If you knew that the clients who want the product or service you offer using your gifts and talents are waiting after you reach one hundred prospects who have declined, devalued, or refused your offer, can you move forward in your pursuit of at least one hundred?

It's important that we holistically accept the reality that failing is often an integral piece of the puzzle that creates the incredible picture of our bright and amazing future if we do not exchange a failed concept or idea for a sentence to eternally live a failed life.

Sometimes a failed situation is not a result of a bad idea but of poor preparation or implementation of that idea. What's worse is when similar situations continue to yield the same outcome, but the individual doesn't stop to truly grasp the fullness of what has occurred from beginning to end to ascertain how to correct the gaps.

For example, if I own a bakery business but I've had to close two of six locations because of poor financial performance and not generating enough sales, I must stop and ask myself a few questions regarding five strategic components of successful execution: location, people, product, time, and service. Does the location provide ease for my target market to reach my product? Do I have the right talent (people) in the right roles or positions? Does my pricing structure accurately account for the cost and overhead of the operation? Does my team produce the results needed by executing the processes and procedures outlined? Is my team delivering a level of customer service that delightfully engages customers consistently?

If I only blamed my staff for poor execution but I didn't ensure we hired the right people and trained them for the positions, how would I expect to avoid making this same mistake repeatedly? If I expected the level of service provided to customers to always be delightfully engaging but failed to effectively set that expectation with my team, how would they deliver?

Ownership is the key in analyzing a failed situation, business, decision, relationship, and so forth. You must accept ownership of the blind spots or hidden areas that become exposed because of your own ignorance, procrastination, distrust, poor planning, communication, or any combination of these pitfalls or others. Accepting ownership is essential to grow and learn the lessons needed to avoid making the same mistakes repeatedly. Learning from the mistakes of others will also help you to avoid problems that someone else has lived through and been gracious enough to show you how to avoid. It's one thing to make your own mistakes out of sheer naivety, but it is terribly troubling to make mistakes repeatedly because of supreme stubbornness or the ugly giant of pride that doesn't want or allow you to admit when you are wrong about someone or something. Friends, please don't allow pride to be the stumbling block that keeps you in cycles of poor decisions that lead to failed outcomes. Allow the blessed wisdom that comes from failed experiences or those who have already lived beyond them and have a proven, credible track record to help guide you through the challenging times that grow and mature you for the next realm of success and distinguished character.

Day Nine Declaration

I, _____ (*insert full name here*), am excited about my journey to realizing my identity, purpose, and vision by unlocking the gift of love inside me. I embrace the certainty of my bright future that awaits with great expectation for unprecedented levels of wealth and prosperity that I never could have dreamed of. I take authority over my paradigm and condition my mind to visualize, sense, and ascertain success in every failed circumstance, situation, relationship, business, and idea. I look forward to the opportunity to demonstrate my learnings and acquired wisdom in every situation that did not yield the expected outcome. I come out of agreement with every feeling and label of failure and loose the effects of that mind-set in my life. I take full ownership of every decision and choice I have made and accept responsibility for the outcomes of those choices. I come out of agreement with pride and stubbornness and come into agreement with humility and graciousness. I am stronger because of the obstacles and challenges I have overcome, not despite them. I am my own success story! I am accessing my Wealth Success Chamber!

My Success Story Reflection Moments

_____

_____

_____

_____

_____

_____

_____

_____

_____

_____

_____

_____

_____

_____

_____

_____

_____

_____

_____

_____

_____

_____

_____

_____

_____

_____

_____

_____

*I love, respect, and appreciate this about who I am:*_____

My Success Story Reflection Moments

_____

_____

_____

_____

_____

_____

_____

_____

_____

_____

_____

_____

_____

_____

_____

_____

_____

_____

_____

_____

_____

_____

_____

_____

_____

_____

_____

_____

_____

_____

*I love, respect, and appreciate this about who I am:*_____

My Success Story Reflection Moments

_____
_____
_____
_____
_____
_____
_____
_____
_____
_____
_____
_____
_____
_____
_____
_____
_____
_____
_____
_____
_____
_____
_____
_____
_____
_____
_____
_____

*I love, respect, and appreciate this about who I am:*_____

Day 10

Am I Ready to Access My Wealth Success Chamber?

Welcome to day ten of your journey to realizing your identity, purpose, and vision to access your own Wealth Success Chamber! Congratulations on successfully completing the first nine days of your personalized life coaching boot camp. By today, you should be experiencing great joy in your journey, as today is the final chapter of this phase. Wow! Can you believe it's been ten days already? In this moment, please give yourself a pat on the back for sticking with the uncomfortable yet unbelievably rewarding task of uncovering the layers of life, issues, obstacles, hurt, and inadequacy to reveal the marvelous, confident, intelligent, and gifted individual that has always lay within. Truly it takes courage to confront yourself in a way that no one else, other than God himself, can see you. I'm 100 percent proud of you and the progress you have made to radically transform the trajectory of your life from being mediocre at best to being highly successful, fulfilled, and purposeful. As we close out this phase, the final chapter in this journal will discuss success defined and what that entails in your life.

Let's begin by stating your identity, purpose, and vision for your life. In the exercise below, please do not look back at your original definition but only state what comes to mind today and in this very moment.

Identity: Who are you?

_____

_____

_____

_____

_____

_____

_____

Purpose: What did God put you here on earth to do?

_____

_____

_____

_____

_____

_____

_____

Vision: What will you accomplish while here?

_____

_____

_____

_____

_____

_____

_____

Now write down your personal definition of success and wealth for your life. In the space below, be specific and use words that help you see a picture or illustration of each definition.

Success Defined:

_____

_____

_____

_____

_____

_____

_____

Wealth Defined:

_____

_____

_____

_____

_____

_____

_____

Thank you for completing the exercise above. It's so often that, rather than creating our own definition for success and wealth, we rely on or comply with the definitions of others only to realize later that their definition is not and will not ever truly be a match for our own lives. The dictionary definition of success is "the achievement of a desired outcome in a situation." What I love about the actual definition of the word *success* is that it gives ample space and opportunity for each of us to tailor the personal definition of success to our lives, linked directly to the goals that we set and achieve and giving us the ability to demonstrate success in every area of our lives. Embracing this fact as truth means that you must be able to articulate your goals for your life to measure success, which is directly tied to fulfillment and living a purpose-filled life. Wealth is defined as an abundance of valuable resources, possessions, assets, and so forth. Let me ask you a question. How can you create goals for your life without a sense and clear understanding of your identity, purpose, and vision?

As I shared a few chapters ago, I undoubtedly and unapologetically am convinced that God created all people with specific and unique purposes and placed inside them the natural gifts and talents they need to fulfill that purpose. In addition, God created us all with a unique target market of people created to serve and deliver a transformational impact to improve their lives. Friends, please understand that you possess something that specific individuals need to improve their quality of life and increase their ability to live a purpose-filled life. *Everyone* has a target market, but unfortunately, until we have clarity about who that target market includes, we may operate in life trying to serve people who were never designed to "eat from our tables." Or worse, not serving anyone at all, believing that we don't have anything to offer anyone that could add value to their lives. The great news is that, just by going through chapters one through ten, you have taken the first step to gain clarity! One fact I want to share with you is that it doesn't take someone any different from you to achieve unprecedented success and wealth. Everyone has a journey, and that journey has a beginning and a destination. Whether you are at the beginning, in the middle, or near the end of your destined journey, you still have every opportunity to demonstrate success in every area of your life.

It's very important that you complete the exercises below in one sitting. They may take up to an hour to complete, but you will need the space to brainstorm, and it's critical that you allow the creativity to flow in one sitting. We will explore your gifts, talents, and strengths and gain clarity on your target market so that you have a sense of direction to move forward to access your Wealth Success Chamber!

What are your top seven natural gifts/talents (special skills or abilities you've had or acquired since birth)?

1.
2.
3.
4.
5.
6.
7.

What are your strengths (things or tasks that you are energized by that also come with great ease)?

1.
2.
3.
4.
5.
6.
7.

In the Wealth Success Chamber Strategy Map below, please combine and select your top seven gifts and strengths first.

Next, brainstorm streams: business or income-generating ideas that can result from the gifts you have selected. I have included an example chart below for your reference. Feel free to use any of the ideas that you believe also apply to you!

Name: _____

Wealth Success Chamber Strategy Map

Gifts/Strengths	Stream Idea 1	Stream Idea 2	Stream Idea 3
Speaking	Keynote	Talk Show	Radio/Podcast
Writing	Books	Cards	Blogs
Coaching	Small Groups	1:1	Workshops
Training	Leadership	Career Planning	Life Skills
Consulting	Small Business	Churches	Schools
Empowerment	Conferences	Mentoring	Youth Classes
Music	Songwriting	Arrangement	Producer

Name: _____

My Wealth Success Chamber Strategy Map

Gifts/Strengths	Stream Idea 1	Stream Idea 2	Stream Idea 3

Gifts/Strengths: Top 3	Partner Needed	1st Step: Research	2nd Step: Resource

What is the greatest lesson you have learned in life that you share with others?

_____

_____

_____

_____

_____

_____

_____

What is the greatest source of pain and hurt in your life that you have learned from? How did you recover from it?

_____

_____

_____

_____

_____

_____

_____

What advice would you give to your younger self that you wish you'd had then?

_____

_____

_____

_____

_____

_____

How would you describe a day in your ideal life?

_____
_____
_____
_____
_____
_____
_____
_____

What is the greatest obstacle that exists today that has prevented you from living your ideal life?

_____
_____
_____
_____
_____
_____
_____
_____

What is the greatest threat to your success?

_____
_____
_____
_____
_____
_____
_____
_____
_____

What are you willing to sacrifice to achieve success?

_____

_____

_____

_____

_____

_____

_____

_____

_____

What are you willing to change in your life to achieve success?

_____

_____

_____

_____

_____

_____

_____

_____

How are you going to rid yourself of all negativity and toxicity and find positive, likeminded individuals to support you during this next phase of your life?

_____

_____

_____

_____

_____

_____

_____

_____

How are you going to allocate your time differently to achieve the goals you have just established while still leaving time for your current responsibilities?

_____

_____

_____

_____

_____

_____

_____

_____

My Success Story Reflection Moments

_____

_____

_____

_____

_____

_____

_____

_____

_____

_____

_____

_____

_____

_____

_____

_____

_____

_____

_____

_____

_____

_____

_____

_____

_____

_____

_____

_____

_____

_____

_____

_____

_____

*I love, respect, and appreciate this about who I am:*_____

My Success Story Reflection Moments

_____
_____
_____
_____
_____
_____
_____
_____
_____
_____
_____
_____
_____
_____
_____
_____
_____
_____
_____
_____
_____
_____
_____
_____
_____
_____
_____
_____
_____

*I love, respect, and appreciate this about who I am:*_____

My Success Story Reflection Moments

_____

_____

_____

_____

_____

_____

_____

_____

_____

_____

_____

_____

_____

_____

_____

_____

_____

_____

_____

_____

_____

_____

_____

_____

_____

_____

_____

_____

*I love, respect, and appreciate this about who I am:*_____

Next Steps: My Action List

1. Identify your Wealth Success Chamber strategy for the next 12 months.
   a. This strategy should be holistic and include every area of your life: personal, financial, family, physical, career, spiritual, etc., and include measurable goals
      i. Select up to four different activities that will add wealth and success to your life as you pursue your purpose and destiny
         1. Use your strengths, interests, talents
         2. Keep in mind that you don't have to be *great* to start, but you *must start* to become *great!*
      ii. My recommendation is to use a SMART model
         1. Specific, measurable, attainable, realistic, time-bound
   b. In your strategy, please include three specific actions you will take consistently to demonstrate your commitment to experience the transformation that already has been accessed in the past 10 days but will need to be actualized.

i. For example, if your financial strategy includes saving money or eliminating debt, your three actions may be as follows:
1. Eliminate all credit card use with exception of emergency use, and commit to pay 2 or 3 times the minimum payment amount
2. Limit eating out (fast food or restaurants) to once per month
3. Identify and pay off one debt per month until all debt is paid
  c. Identify an accountability partner to share your 12-month strategy and monthly updates on your progress
    i. Trusted friend or mentor
2. Research the partners and resources needed to fulfill your strategy
3. Seek out opportunities to gain further knowledge, exposure, etc., in your gifts or talents
  a. Research and subscribe to newsletters, articles, videos, conferences, calls, trainings, etc.
  b. Don't dismiss opportunities to invest in yourself
    i. Every learning opportunity will not be free
4. Be intentional about learning from *every failed experience*
  a. Expect everything *not* to always go as planned, and prepare and position your mind to be ready to see the lesson behind every situation that you experience, whether successful or "failed." The key is that you will probably learn your most valuable lessons from the failed experiences versus the successful ones. Every failed opportunity better positions you to *win* greater gains in the upcoming experience if *you are willing* to learn and grow and perform differently as a result of what you have learned

    b. *Never stop trying*

5. Fully commit to unlocking the gift of love inside you by embracing your 100 percent authentic self.
   a. Rid yourself of all negative self-talk
   b. Reassess your relationships, and rid yourself of any relationships that are not value adding but are toxic or negative
   c. Challenge yourself daily to increase your appreciation for and adoration of the person you are and are becoming
   d. Enjoy your alone time
   e. Take lunch and dinner dates alone to truly embrace and enjoy your own company

6. Fully commit to moving outside of your comfort zone weekly
   a. Perform an activity that stretches you outside of your "norm." This may include your normal friends, places, activities, etc.
   b. Be present (alert, engaged, all in) during this activity, and recognize your progress with every new and uncomfortable activity
   c. Don't be so hard on yourself! You will make mistakes, but remember to learn from those mistakes and become better because of, not despite them

For day ten and our final declaration in this first phase of transformation, I am going to ask you to write out the affirmation in the space below. Please take as much time as you need to truly impart the declaration below using positive and value-adding statements about you, your accomplishments, and your journey that lies ahead. I am extremely proud of all the progress you have made and of the successful journey you've made to realize your identity, purpose, and vision to access your Wealth Success Chamber. Holistically, you should now be experiencing more abundance in every area of your life since you have begun to rid yourself of toxicity. Always remember to protect your peace, liberty, clarity, joy, positivity, aspirations, contentment, and satisfaction by maintaining an environment that invites only those attributes. Anything or anyone that doesn't support your transformation is no longer welcome to take residence in your life. Continue moving forward, and be the *amazingly wealthy, successful, and prosperous* individual you were created to be.

I look forward to hearing your success stories, as *you are a success story*! Contact me at **www.wealthsuccesschamber.com** to share! Godspeed, and God bless you!

I, _____ (*insert your name here*), am excited about my journey to realizing my identity, purpose, and vision by unlocking the gift of love inside me.

_____

_____

_____

_____

_____

_____

_____

_____

_____

I am accessing my Wealth Success Chamber!

My Success Story Implementation Strategy

_____
_____
_____
_____
_____
_____
_____
_____
_____
_____
_____
_____
_____
_____
_____
_____
_____
_____
_____
_____
_____
_____
_____
_____
_____
_____
_____
_____
_____

*I love, respect, and appreciate this about who I am:*_____

My Success Story Implementation Strategy

_____
_____
_____
_____
_____
_____
_____
_____
_____
_____
_____
_____
_____
_____
_____
_____
_____
_____
_____
_____
_____
_____
_____
_____
_____
_____
_____
_____
_____
_____

*I love, respect, and appreciate this about who I am:*_____

My Success Story Implementation Strategy

_____
_____
_____
_____
_____
_____
_____
_____
_____
_____
_____
_____
_____
_____
_____
_____
_____
_____
_____
_____
_____
_____
_____
_____
_____
_____
_____
_____
_____
_____

*I love, respect, and appreciate this about who I am:*_____

My Success Story Implementation Strategy

_____
_____
_____
_____
_____
_____
_____
_____
_____
_____
_____
_____
_____
_____
_____
_____
_____
_____
_____
_____
_____
_____
_____
_____
_____
_____
_____
_____

*I love, respect, and appreciate this about who I am:*_____

My Success Story Implementation Strategy

_____
_____
_____
_____
_____
_____
_____
_____
_____
_____
_____
_____
_____
_____
_____
_____
_____
_____
_____
_____
_____
_____
_____
_____
_____
_____
_____
_____
_____

*I love, respect, and appreciate this about who I am:*_____

My Success Story Implementation Strategy

_____
_____
_____
_____
_____
_____
_____
_____
_____
_____
_____
_____
_____
_____
_____
_____
_____
_____
_____
_____
_____
_____
_____
_____
_____
_____
_____
_____
_____
_____

*I love, respect, and appreciate this about who I am:*_____

My Success Story Implementation Strategy

_____
_____
_____
_____
_____
_____
_____
_____
_____
_____
_____
_____
_____
_____
_____
_____
_____
_____
_____
_____
_____
_____
_____
_____
_____
_____
_____
_____
_____
_____
_____

*I love, respect, and appreciate this about who I am:*_____

My Success Story Implementation Strategy

_____
_____
_____
_____
_____
_____
_____
_____
_____
_____
_____
_____
_____
_____
_____
_____
_____
_____
_____
_____
_____
_____
_____
_____
_____
_____
_____
_____
_____
_____

*I love, respect, and appreciate this about who I am:*_____

My Success Story Implementation Strategy

_____
_____
_____
_____
_____
_____
_____
_____
_____
_____
_____
_____
_____
_____
_____
_____
_____
_____
_____
_____
_____
_____
_____
_____
_____
_____
_____
_____

*I love, respect, and appreciate this about who I am:*_____

My Success Story Implementation Strategy

_____
_____
_____
_____
_____
_____
_____
_____
_____
_____
_____
_____
_____
_____
_____
_____
_____
_____
_____
_____
_____
_____
_____
_____
_____
_____
_____
_____
_____

*I love, respect, and appreciate this about who I am:*_____

My Success Story Implementation Strategy

_____
_____
_____
_____
_____
_____
_____
_____
_____
_____
_____
_____
_____
_____
_____
_____
_____
_____
_____
_____
_____
_____
_____
_____
_____
_____
_____
_____
_____

*I love, respect, and appreciate this about who I am:*_____

My Success Story Implementation Strategy

_____
_____
_____
_____
_____
_____
_____
_____
_____
_____
_____
_____
_____
_____
_____
_____
_____
_____
_____
_____
_____
_____
_____
_____
_____
_____
_____
_____
_____

*I love, respect, and appreciate this about who I am:*_____

My Success Story Implementation Strategy

_____

_____

_____

_____

_____

_____

_____

_____

_____

_____

_____

_____

_____

_____

_____

_____

_____

_____

_____

_____

_____

_____

_____

_____

_____

_____

_____

_____

_____

*I love, respect, and appreciate this about who I am:*_____

My Success Story Implementation Strategy

_____

_____

_____

_____

_____

_____

_____

_____

_____

_____

_____

_____

_____

_____

_____

_____

_____

_____

_____

_____

_____

_____

_____

_____

_____

_____

_____

_____

_____

_____

_____

_____

_____

*I love, respect, and appreciate this about who I am:*_____

My Success Story Implementation Strategy

_____
_____
_____
_____
_____
_____
_____
_____
_____
_____
_____
_____
_____
_____
_____
_____
_____
_____
_____
_____
_____
_____
_____
_____
_____
_____
_____
_____

*I love, respect, and appreciate this about who I am:*_____

My Success Story Implementation Strategy

_____

_____

_____

_____

_____

_____

_____

_____

_____

_____

_____

_____

_____

_____

_____

_____

_____

_____

_____

_____

_____

_____

_____

_____

_____

_____

_____

_____

_____

*I love, respect, and appreciate this about who I am:*_____

My Success Story Implementation Strategy

_____

_____

_____

_____

_____

_____

_____

_____

_____

_____

_____

_____

_____

_____

_____

_____

_____

_____

_____

_____

_____

_____

_____

_____

_____

_____

_____

_____

_____

*I love, respect, and appreciate this about who I am:*_____

My Success Story Implementation Strategy

_____
_____
_____
_____
_____
_____
_____
_____
_____
_____
_____
_____
_____
_____
_____
_____
_____
_____
_____
_____
_____
_____
_____
_____
_____
_____
_____
_____
_____
_____

*I love, respect, and appreciate this about who I am:*_____

My Success Story Implementation Strategy

_____

_____

_____

_____

_____

_____

_____

_____

_____

_____

_____

_____

_____

_____

_____

_____

_____

_____

_____

_____

_____

_____

_____

_____

_____

_____

_____

_____

_____

_____

_____

_____

_____

_____

*I love, respect, and appreciate this about who I am:*_____

My Success Story Implementation Strategy

_____

_____

_____

_____

_____

_____

_____

_____

_____

_____

_____

_____

_____

_____

_____

_____

_____

_____

_____

_____

_____

_____

_____

_____

_____

_____

_____

_____

_____

*I love, respect, and appreciate this about who I am:*_____

My Success Story Implementation Strategy

_____
_____
_____
_____
_____
_____
_____
_____
_____
_____
_____
_____
_____
_____
_____
_____
_____
_____
_____
_____
_____
_____
_____
_____
_____

*I love, respect, and appreciate this about who I am:*_____

My Success Story Implementation Strategy

_____
_____
_____
_____
_____
_____
_____
_____
_____
_____
_____
_____
_____
_____
_____
_____
_____
_____
_____
_____
_____
_____
_____
_____
_____
_____
_____

*I love, respect, and appreciate this about who I am:*_____

My Success Story Implementation Strategy

_____

_____

_____

_____

_____

_____

_____

_____

_____

_____

_____

_____

_____

_____

_____

_____

_____

_____

_____

_____

_____

_____

_____

_____

_____

_____

_____

_____

_____

_____

_____

_____

_____

_____

*I love, respect, and appreciate this about who I am:*_____

My Success Story Implementation Strategy

_____
_____
_____
_____
_____
_____
_____
_____
_____
_____
_____
_____
_____
_____
_____
_____
_____
_____
_____
_____
_____
_____
_____
_____
_____
_____
_____
_____
_____
_____
_____

*I love, respect, and appreciate this about who I am:*_____